great

america

Also by James McManus

Ghost Waves
Curtains
Chin Music
Out of the Blue

great

america

poems

james mcmanus

HarperPerennial
A Division of HarperCollinsPublishers

Poems from this collection have appeared, sometimes in different versions, in *American Poetry Review, Antioch Review, The Atlantic Monthly, Columbia Poetry Review, Fortnight* (Belfast), *Harvard Magazine, The Honest Ulsterman* (Belfast and London), *Kansas Quarterly, New American Writing, New Directions, No Roses Review, Other Voices, Parnassus, P-Form, The Salmon* (Galway), *Sou'Wester, Spoon River Poetry Review, TXT* (Paris), and *Wire.*

"Smash and Scatteration" was reprinted in *The Best American Poetry 1991.*

"Bacon Dance" was produced in 1990 as a broadside by Artists Bookworks, with art by Raymond Martin, and was subsequently published in *Another Chicago Magazine.*

A condensed version (sections 1, 3, 15, 16, 28, and 31) of "Great America" appeared in a special issue of *Parnassus* on the American Long Poem; section 23 appeared, as "23", in *Antioch Review;* section 9 appeared, as "2 Live Soul", in *Clockwatch Review.*

The author is grateful to the editors of these magazines and anthologies, as well as to the Ford Foundation, the National Endowment for the Arts, the Shifting Foundation, the Illinois Arts Council, and Arts International for their generous support while this work was in progress.

HarperCollins books may be purchased for educational, business, or sales promotional use. For information please write: Special Markets Department, HarperCollins Publishers, Inc., 10 East 53rd Street, New York, NY 10022.

FIRST EDITION

Designed by Alma Hochhauser Orenstein

Library of Congress Cataloging-in-Publication Data
McManus, James
    Great America : poems / by James McManus.—1st ed.
      p.   cm.
    ISBN 0-06-055347-2 / ISBN 0-06-096994-6 (pbk.)
    I. Title.
    PS3563.C386G74   1993   92-54851
811'.54—dc20

93 94 95 96 97 CC/HC 10 9 8 7 6 5 4 3 2 1
93 94 95 96 97 CC/HC 10 9 8 7 6 5 4 3 2 1 (pbk.)

one

Centrifuge: Islets of Langerhans   *5*

Triptych   *7*

Twelfth Night   *12*

My Father's Sunglasses   *13*

Counting Her Syllables Before They're Hatched   *14*

Carpenter Enzyme   *15*

Post Dance   *16*

Bacon Dance   *17*

Gespensterwellen   *20*

Hubbard Woods   *22*

two

Slash Art   *27*

Smash and Scatteration   *35*

Wisconsin   *47*

three

Great America   *57*

one

Success is counted sweetest
By those who ne'er succeed.
To comprehend a nectar
Requires sorest need.

Not one of all the purple Host
Who took the Flag today
Can tell the definition
So clear of Victory

As he defeated—dying—
On whose forbidden ear
The distant strains of triumph
Burst agonized and clear!

—EMILY DICKINSON

CENTRIFUGE: ISLETS OF LANGERHANS

It's 8:01 of an evening. Instead of "So What"
or "Blood Sugar Sex Magik," which, as it happens,
are both on this house-mix cassette, here I am half

listening to Maria Callas sing Massenet's "Air
de Chimène" while I read, riveted, in *The Times*
about researchers' efforts to cure diabetes.

Transplanting an entire unwieldy used pancreas
is no longer necessary. Now only the actual
insulin-producing cells, called islets of Langerhans,

are taken, separated out from the donor pancreatic
tissue in a centrifuge, yielding a bagful of what
"looks like pink grapefruit juice." This potent

solution gets dripped directly through the portal
vein into the patient's liver, where, about two
hours later, the islets begin to make insulin.

But. The procedure will not be available "for three
to five years, except"—except?—"to patients already
requiring transplants of other organs," which even

at this stage of things leaves me out. And there's more
downside: daily injections of FK 506,
an immunosuppressant derived from a Japanese

fungus, will have to be substituted for (in
my case, twice-daily) injections of insulin. So.
Since my xenophobic body accepts nothing foreign,

and, brother, I mean *nothing* . . . It already zapped
its own perfectly functional islets of Langerhans
twenty-six years ago, somehow mistaking the seventeen

amino acids on their surface for the almost *not*
quite identical configuration on bovine serum
albumen. Cow's milk. And all because Mom didn't nurse me. . . .

It's time to test my blood, do my shot, have some dinner,
for which I imperiously decide to get naked. My
islets don't work, so I'll not eat tonight with my clothes on!

I use the remote thing to turn up the music to nine.
Ms. Callas isn't done singing quite yet. I do dumb
little jigs while I lip-sync, then stand still and listen.

My blood, liquid glass, oozes from deep in my gut
to the tip of my left middle finger, which now I must prick.
I spin myself round maybe six, seven times, and kick

off my underpants. Catch them. The bass of "So What" is
buzzing my woofers. When Miles finally hits it I'm turning
again, breathing and shivering hard, getting dizzy.

1

When Pinnock recorded the *Goldberg Variations* at the Paris
Conservatoire in 1980 on a Ruckers two-manual harpsichord
he omitted the repeats in both statements of the Aria

as well as—get this—in Variations 3, 7,
9, 12, 13, 15, 17, 21,
24, 25, and 29—or so

Moira informed me. Glenn Gould's baffled, sotto
voce yodeling, during both his '81
Yamaha and '55 Steinway renditions

did not annoy Moira all that
much, though she certainly
in no way approved, let me

tell you. She did love to have to explain how it was
that Bach's patron, Count Hermann Carl von Kayserlingk
something something IV, commissioned the work

so that his court harpsichordist, Johann Gottlieb
Goldberg, could help to alleviate Count Hermann's
almost terminal insomnia. She would often go on

to deconstruct à la Derrida the G major "Sarabande"
bass theme: how it patently derived from the second
1725 Anna Magdalena Notebook, was comprised as

a simulacrum of two sixteen-bar sections, and was
constructed symmetrically, coming to a half close
then returning by way of E minor to the tonic.

But it was during the sixteenth of the *variationen*
—as she always liked to pronounce them—written
in the style of a French—wink—overture, with its

slow, dotted introduction, as well as in the fugue
that "must" follow, that the binary-Baudrillardian
(de)construction of the work was made most emphatic.

We, the hypnotized public, were thereby as it were
leukemized by the hallucinatory and indeterminate
play of hyperreal signs—or, in the case of Bach,

notes. The music itself was simulated, while the amoeba-
like mutations of the systemic code sustained the—how
did she put it?—illusions of technique and experience.

2

It's so long since I was last with her
Come closer, come closer, come closer

I took her to see Talking Heads on our third date, and it was
After that concert we made decent love for the first and last time

It's been so long since I found out
What people mean by down and out

Other bands she told me she wouldn't mind all that much
        observing
in performance were Juan and Joan Armatrading, ZZ Top and
        the London

Chamber Orchestra on authentic period instruments
conducted by Trevor Pinnock, Bill Frisell and the Paint,

Viktoria Mullova and the Mandellas, Shrimp Boat, Emanuel
Ax and the Attractions, the Blues Magoos, Youssou N'Dour,
        Richard Hell

and the Voidoids, Thomas Pynchon and Laurie Anderson, Jürgen
        Habermas
and the Magic Band, Ronnie Spector and the Sucking Stones,
        Philip Glass

and the Photographers, Don Van Vliet and the South Vietnamese
Regular Army, Ex:No 'N' Ungh, Ronald Shannon Jackson and
        Squeeze,

Eric Dolphy with Slowhand Luke Nagelbach on red-and-white
        Strat,
Chris Spedding and Black Jack McDowell with the Alban Berg
        Quartett,

The Pogues with Shane MacGowan, Ice-T and Nigel Kennedy,
        Public Image Ltd.,
Jesse Helms and the Bleeding Signs of the Cross, Buddy Guy,
        Mr. Ted

Nugent and the Papas, ?Question Mark and the Mysterians, The
    Who
with Paul Muldoon, Power Tools, Kate Bush and the
    Ejaculations, U2

with Rachel Gena on viola, Miles Davis and Maria Callas, the
    Cagey Radio
Radios, Glen Campbell and The Blacks Unlimited, Mr. Claudio

Abbado conducting CSO, Souled American, Al Green and the
    Yellow
Bellied Sapsuckers, my mother and The Mothers of Invention,
    Yo-Yo

Ma and Yo Mama, John E. Stopford and the Spiders from Mars,
Charles Mingus and Foday Musa Suso, the Art Thieves, The
    Cars,

Janis Ian, The Yardbirds, John Coltrane, Tone Loc and the
    Wolfe Tones,
the Kronos Quartet and Hamza El Din, and Van Morrison and
    the Chieftains.

But I couldn't find a Ticketmaster that took my Discover
and neither could Moira so that was about it, pretty much.

The thing is *Oh muscles flex and fingers curl*
And a cold sweat breaks out on a sweater girl

It's so long since I was last with her
It's strict time

It was cabbage and turnips that drove her away
Had my mother cooked meat she'd've opted to stay

Come closer, come closer
Come closer

3

When I can't fall asleep, I never
count sheep. I count all the things that I love
about Moira, *dum dum dum dum dum*. I also remember
her surprise fortieth birthday party. She got mostly dumb
joke presents, things like aviator sunglasses, a tame strip
by a rented Chippendale with acne on his back, handsome
handstitched gray herringbone Donegal tweed bikini
panties—"a G cozy," their designer, Aurora Bernini,
one of her several not unattractive Lesbian colleagues,
had dubbed them—and a bottle of forty-year-old scotch.
Whatever is left of that scotch is now forty-two. So's
Moira. They'll continue to be the same age, I suppose,
for as long as any of either is left. Till either
is gone. Till nothing is left of the other.

The skin on my legs itched and tingled as I draped my damp socks
over the crosscountry-skiing machine Moira had got us for Christmas.
About the only thing we'd used it for so far was a clothes rack
and, once, as a not entirely successful marital aid. It was
starting to remind me of a high-tech but lonely mechanical reindeer,
cut from its herd of frisky girl reindeer, sold into exercise slavery
and summarily UPSed from Lapland across the North Pole to Wilmette,
only to be parked ignominiously, with sweat socks and lingerie
hung from its antlers, in the corner of some lazy slobs' bedroom.
Postmodern exercise guilt, I supposed, as I tossed my Gitanos
onto the sawed-off teak skis—although from certain angles it did
sort of look like a reindeer, at least about as much as Picasso's
old bicycle saddle and handlebars looked like a bull's head.
I stood there just holding my T-shirt and Jockeys, and shivered.

MY FATHER'S SUNGLASSES

The best things in life are pink. My father
informed me of this twenty-six years ago. We were waiting
in front of the awningless First Bank of Lisle for my mother.
It was Saturday morning, late June or early July, and blindingly
sunny, even with my cap pulled down low. And it's hotter than
       hell,
said my father. He had on a T-shirt and sweatstained tortoiseshell
sunglasses. I was wearing my polyester Bronco League uniform
and clutching a brand-new green passbook in my first-baseman's
       mitt.
My savings account had one line, $60.00, money I'd got
from relatives for my eighth-grade graduation, plus
some I'd made as a caddie. I was rich, I thought
then, but I'd started to feel kind of nervous.
We were gonna be late for my game, and I had no idea
what my father was talking about.

COUNTING HER SYLLABLES BEFORE
THEY'RE HATCHED

Moira Macomber's rifle doesn't actually
kill people—*es dadora de imagenes*. Okay?

Her T-shirted figure does feature a photograph of Samuel
      Beckett
silkscreened on top of a block of the Sucking Stones

passage from the Tetralogy, and yet as I'm cracking this egg
and writing these syllables Merit smoke plumes from my nostrils

or would have plumed had I been writing them
a hundred and seventeen hours ago, *una danza*

de chispas entre las bleedin' letras,
una fuga de vocales en fuego as

I masticate toothpicks with the Zanes brothers'
"Don't Run Wild," jingle bells and all, on 11, my singed fingers

corriendo sobre cenizas calcinadas
because the side of this page is on fire.

CARPENTER ENZYME

Ankleted, gumsnapping mama
flashes green, swerving

Mesopotamian eyes
alongside the boisterous

psychotic you see
twice a week on this El

backwashing into his Pepsi
not thinking to offer you any:

okay. But thirteen-year-olds
in ivory boudoirwear

pout from a damp, wrinkled
billboard at Dearborn

and—what is this?
Lake. And their child.

POST DANCE

slowly
on tiptoe

    let them brush
    your rock and roll hair

held fast
by the nipples

    let them leave you
    up in the air

held fast
but slowly

    butt clenching
    and kissing

not kissing
on tiptoe

BACON DANCE

Face in the paste-
spattered mirror

an uncombed grenade
all set to go off.

Bowel ditto. Neon blue
water, used tissue.

Unzipped, without warning,
reproductive organs

levitate, buzz, past appendix
as floor plunges twenty-nine

stories, funny bone
wings something hard.

Not really scared
shitless exactly, more

a dead tired, unmitered
bishop's prick of dis-

combobulation: pants
down, off balance, in this

the executive-class
john of an Aer Lingus

747
encountering sudden

bronco turbulence. NO SMOKING
RETURN TO SEAT IMMEDIATELY

But there you are: kneecapped
by handle of tampon disposal,

not smoking, what's left of charcoal
left lung hawked up wrong pipe

to begin with, doing your best
to take closest seat or, better, stand up.

No dice. The plane goes diagonal
along two or three axes, splaying

your balancing hand in the mung
of the sink. Something bangs

down below, doesn't
sound right.

Terrorist
boombox

lined with two
pounds of Semtex?

Your own new
aluminum suitcase

retrofitted in Shannon
by someone whose . . . Captain's

voice over toilet intercom
like mated pair of killer

Ethiopian cheetahs
in Phoenix Park Zoo: Cool and Calm.

Outside, impossibly, a
contrail slides by the extra

six hours of blasted gray
moon rising over Good Friday

as sparks flint
along your flexed sole

and your plastic
windowless asshole

gets smaller
and smaller.

GESPENSTERWELLEN

What's a ghost? I overhear him say
with tingling energy. One word
or less. One who will *not fade away*

through radical time or chord
changes, bad manners, or death.
Not even from too-minty breath.

Plus that weird Alec Guinness
premonition, or early déjà
vu, that James Dean totals his Porsche

at noon the afternoon before
it happens? Good
reason for Shane to drink Guinness.

Photographing, dating, painting
or naming ghosts helps, but once
she waves bye-bye everything

follows with most unfair
certainty, like a prayer
almost, goosing the market for art

stars. Take Moira's fisheater farts
in the kitchen or, worse, under
our blue Ramberg quilt: void where

prohibited. Women!
Those richards! Those wearers of certain
underwear! I mean how *dare* they?

Yet such things do have a way
of turning out to be pretty
much what we will make of them

anyway. Like am I wanton
or wanted or wonton
I wonder. I cancer us

in Japanese, I'm on my knees
to cancel us. But please
don't be putting my pretty

big head into that little git hat
just yet. I've done my duty,
Mack, so that's enough of that.

Face it. I'm grotty. My hair's way
too long. Paint it black, '69,
speedballs and crunchy. Amen.

HUBBARD WOODS

I saw it.
A thing that was cold and dry.
It was me.

two

Then I went back into the house and wrote, It is midnight. The rain is beating on the windows. It was not midnight. It was not raining.

—Samuel Beckett, *Molloy*

SLASH ART

is verbal slash visual.
It recombines pictures, moving

and otherwise, with language
in ways that can make things

make new kinds of sense. Performative
for the most part, it incorporates between

two and five dimensions, time being
perhaps the most significant, and north

of the Tropic of Cancer will constitute what serious
artists tend to produce well into the third millennium

anno Domini, when something else will happen. In the meantime
people who read books, employ good old fugal procedure, and
            understand rules

can change quickly will make much more
interesting art, and much much more money. Picasso

was a Slash Artist, particularly between
1909 and 1913, and one

of the best, if only on the basis of *Still
Life with Chair Caning.* He was not very tall

and mistreated women and kids. A Republican
of sorts, he purchased tweedy wardrobes, villas, women

even, with left-handed doodles on checks,
though he seldom drew hickeys on necks.

Picasso's has lately been a common case
with all the Lakers in and out of place:

Worthy's mute kowtowing to Michael
Jordan for Wheaties, Kareem's farewell

tour of every last stadium as the Aging Giant *eeoo!*
Chocolate Ant, Cooper and Scott as these like New

Age Family Guys, slick Pat Riley's annual arrival at the
        Madhouse
on Madison (entering tiny but famous

Gate 3½ after strolling past The Man
in the Dark Suit's fire engine

scarlet Testarossa with the M
AIR J North

Carolina vanity plates)
to provide, if nothing else, young girls a slick Pat

to ogle, Magic buying up radio stations, and speaking
of whom, as my just-off-the-plane South Korean

students are wont to ask politely: sir, if in
the parlance of African Americans your johnson

is your penis, and magic means, uh, magic . . .
I tell them to remember John Sylvester, whom Byron

facetiously claimed lay claim to have lain
with Ben Jonson's sister, prompting Jonson

to claim to have lain with Sir Sylvester's wife,
and that the difference between Jonson and Johnson

can be Slash Art. Examples I give when I'm soberer
include "Tangled Up in Blue" recorded live, in one take, in a
        Lower

East Side studio, or Jenny Holzer's well-made granite benches
        and di-
ode boards proclaiming things like PROTECT ME FROM WHAT I
    WANT and MY

BABYSITTER IS PREGNANT AND THINGS ARE A MESS. For other
        people's money nothing
beats post-Beat badass poet Jerome Sala himself of an evening

at St. Mark's Church in the Bowery, say, in burnt Norton
autumn umber AMVETS bowling shirtsleeves reciting in unfake
        Chicago

Polack his poem about sniffing tic and dating
his brother when his girlfriend's on the rag

or his earlier masterwork, "I Beat Up Willem de Kooning,"
    knowing
as we watch and listen that he (Jerome) has spent the morning
    writing

advertising copy for Time Incorporated, is actually Stuart
Dybek's second cousin, that sixteen years ago he broke his right
    foot

dancing too hard with a Medusa-haired woman
called Bambi who, at the time, was, like

Jerome, addicted to heroin and alcohol, but
also knowing he's currently clean (he writes,

after all, for Time Inc.) and is happily married
to Elaine Equi, the talented Catholic

miniaturist poet. The point is that smarts
and juxtaposition and timing, in Slash Art,

are critical. Some other examples: Godard's *Sympathy
for the Devil,* Jonathan Waterbury's upside down

727, Borofsky's *I dreamed I was taller than Picasso
at 2,047,324* or *Running Man*

on the Berlin Wall at 2,511,898,
Billie Holiday creaking through "I'll Be Around"

then dying three days after Bastille Day, O'Hara and Rivers's
poetry-and-paint collaborations, Lin Hixson's gee-whizz

attack choreography and tribunal vocals, Alastair MacLennon's
homeless performances, Roz Chasts and Glen Baxters, just about
      everything Johns

painted before Nixon resigned, *A Love Supreme,* Braque's hungry
beige and nervous umber *Homage to J. S. Bach,* Fang

MacGowan bar-chording a yellow Telecaster while scorching
      and snarling "Poor Paddy"
and "Transmetropolitan" on St. Patrick's Night at the Brixton
      Academy,

Bacon's early throbbing-gristle triptychs, J. S. G. Boggs's
spending of his own hand-drawn twenties . . . What it isn't is

any old handjob during which the tenderer groans some
sweet nothing your way *Like anybody home?*

or some squinting and mumbling dipster with triceps like Jell-O
dessert treats the purple

crack of whose buttocks are succinctly revealed
above these Caribbean green

Sears Best work pants
as he tends to your quaint little village's errant

toiletry.
It might be

an undrugged, sober Mick Jagger, the erstwhile
yelping whirling

dervish, hawking
Budweiser (this after he began to remember whatever it was

he learned at that fucking London School of Economics)
or, more likely, grunting—drugged, drunk—against the ornery
        opening licks

in Keith's famous open-G tuning
of "Can't You Hear Me Knocking?"

Or what about the way Chrissie Hynde
and John Milton's notion of time

as avenger potently informs the ticking, pendular, slashing
guitar work of Robbie McIntosh on two-thirds of *Learning*

to Crawl can't but help us both forget
and remember James Honeyman-Scott?

I conclude this manifesto
with a passage from Samuel Beckett, who died, at 83, two
        Fridays ago

in a Montparnasse hospital. Born an Irish Protestant
in Stillorgan, Dublin, on Good Friday, the thirteenth

of April, 1906, Mr. Beckett claimed to the end to remember a
        lot of the time
he had spent, during Lent, in the womb.

He wrote
in French and English. He and his wife

had no children
and mistreated no one. In *Endgame,*

Hamm, Beckett's fierce, trenchant Lear-figure, will die soon
and knows it. He is blind and in very great pain

and hears blood
dripping inside his head.

In toque and dark glasses, he sits in a thronelike wheelchair
and haughtily begs for toy dogs, an audience, reports on the
        weather

and time. Near the end of the play's single act he desperately
        asks, for
the fifth and last time, "Is it not time for my painkiller?"

Clov, his bony and demented manservant, son, and witness,
who should always be played by a talented mime, proclaims,
        "Yes."

Hamm: "Ah! At last! Give it to me! Quick!"
After a pause, Clov announces, "There's no more painkiller."

Hamm is appalled
but says, "Good!

No more painkiller!" Clov: "No more painkiller.
You'll never get any more painkiller."

Hamm: "But the little round box. It was full!"
Clov: "Yes. But now it's empty."

A pause before Hamm asks him quietly, "What'll I do?"
When he gets no response he shrieks, "What'll I do?"

Clov, satisfied, begins to move about the skull-like
set, ignoring him, searching for an alarm clock.

SMASH AND SCATTERATION

1

About a year and a half ago my then girlfriend
Linda's parents came home from an Eric Burdon
concert and found QT, their thirteen-week-old

black Labrador retriever, dead on the floor
of the living room, his muzzle lodged—locked
—inside a box of Screaming Yellow Zonkers.

The TV was on, since QT always liked to hear
human voices when Linda's parents went out
without him for more than a couple of minutes.

A young Chinese man in a gleaming white shirt
was standing in front of a tank. Linda told me
her mother was struck by the fact that QT's hungry

asphyxiation had probably caused him
to suffer, and that when the camera panned back
there were fourteen or fifteen more tanks.

2

Last month my great-aunt committed suicide
by jumping from her eighty-second-story bedroom
window. Her third husband had recently died

and she had been suffering from Alzheimer's
disease and cervical cancer. She apparently smashed
through the triple-ply glass with a miniature

dumbbell, put down the dumbbell and thought
about things for a while, then stepped out the hole.
Buffeted furiously by the Venturi Effect,

she bounced down the sunny south side of her
building, the Hancock, for almost twelve seconds.
When she finally hit the sidewalk on Delaware

her gray head snapped off and caromed back up
in the air. According to three gore-bespattered
eyewitnesses, the wicked backspin imparted

3

to her head by the impact made it kick
back up toward the Hancock in a kind of
American twist. Chris Burden fired a pistol

at a 747. I watched Linda's face
while she watched him. In shorts but no shirt,
Picasso drew nudes with a light pen. Mick Jagger

put on a suit, slicked back his hair, and taunted
some corporate nancies. Chris Burden had himself shot
in the left biceps with a .22 caliber

copper-jacketed slug. Three young men brandishing
automatic weapons burst in on an opening
at the Randolph Street Gallery and kidnapped

a frail-looking elderly gentleman by placing
the muzzle of an Ingram MAC-10 to his gums
and walking him out the door backward. On

4

that evening's news, between Gorbymania
stories, the elderly gentleman allegedly turned
out to have been a confederate, the weapons

authentic. A skinny little guy with black hair
stood his ground as fifteen tanks tried to advance.
In shorts and no shirt, Picasso drew nudes

with a cigarette. Timothy Mostert drew witheringly
sardonic caricatures of me while he was supposed
to be listening to, and indeed taking notes on, my

lecture on *Endgame*. During the concert he gave
while QT was gorging himself, Eric Burdon
exhibited his denim-clad crotch in a provocative

manner. Two nights ago, on the David Letterman
show, Kevin Costner, the father of four, exhibited
his denim-clad crotch in a provocative manner.

5

A handsome black model arrested for gang rape
and murder, when some scar-faced honky trash
were the culprits, kissed Madonna. Blood oozed

from wooden facsimiles of his model brown eyes.
He was innocent! Sporting stigmata and backlit
by twelve burning crosses, a brunette Madonna

shimmied lasciviously. Boy! Dred Scott Tyler
placed the American flag on the floor of a gallery.
On the wall perpendicular to the flag

were a notebook and pen along with black-and-white
photographs implying virulent third-world abhorrence
of imperialist behavior perpetrated under

or in the name of the flag. It was convenient
but not really necessary to stand on the flag
while writing comments in the notebook. Other than

6

written responses were implicitly, some averred
illicitly, invited by Tyler's provocative title:
What Is the Proper Way to Display the U.S. Flag?

In *Dick Instruction* two loinclothed men banged a drum
and shot at each other with sixteen-gauge shotguns.
Laurie Anderson had an affair with Thomas Pynchon

and collaborated with William S. Burroughs. Joy Poe
was raped by Pete Panek. The reactions of the audience
were videotaped. Karen Finley signed books in a strip

mall. Jimi Hendrix performed the national anthem
at sunrise. In *The Long Good Friday* the bird what gobbed
on Eric slapped 'Arold (Bob Hoskins) across the face.

Hoskins later retaliated by shredding Eric's froat
with the jagged shards of a bottle of thirty-year-old
Macallan. Eric's jugular was severed and blood spurted

7

onto Hoskins' silk shirt. Lynda Kay died in a snuff film.
Hoskins went home and rinsed off the blood in the shower
while his (dis)loyal moll burned the shirt. Before

receiving her honorary degree from The School
of the Art Institute of Chicago, along with Ed Paschke,
Laurie Anderson had lunch with me in the Ed Muskie

Room of the Congress Hotel. Following Lin Hixson's
instructions, Matt Goulish put on a tutu. Laurie
Anderson stifled a belch with her fist. Her mother, an

avid horsewoman from Wayne, Illinois, had taught her
good manners. Following Lin Hixson's instructions,
Matt Goulish crashed to the floor. David Nelson

painted an average portrait of Harold Washington,
the recently deceased African American mayor
of Chicago, wearing women's lingerie and hung

8

it inside The School of the Art Institute
of Chicago. Tony Jones, The School's new President,
summoned Nelson, a graduating senior, to his wee

windowless office. He requested that Nelson consider
voluntarily removing the painting, if only in order
to avert a potentially violent confrontation

with members of Chicago's African American community,
whose rage had been galvanized by half a dozen African
American aldermen. The interview between the two men

lasted three and a half hours. In the end Nelson turned
down Jones's request, and the painting was confiscated
by Chicago police officers. It turned out later that

day that the young man Jones had been interviewing
was Timothy Mostert, David Nelson's roommate. Chris
Burden resembled Van Morrison. The title

9

of Lin Hixson's performance was *We Got a Date*.
James Fox is beaten and stripped and then beaten again
by belt-wielding cockney mafiosi B. Yeltsin.

Linda Krajacik tunes a gold-top Les Paul, slices
up a pomegranate, performs her new *Bacon Dance*
monologue. An Aer Lingus 747 taxies

to the start of a runway, preparing for takeoff.
An attractive blond flight attendant pretends
to hassle a handsome serviceman for not having

fastened his seat belt. Four feet below her, in
the cargo bay, inside a tan leather suitcase,
is a boombox laden with Semtex. Randy Newman's

best lyric continues to be "Gone Dead Train."
Paul Newman's best dressing continues to be
Creamy Garlic. Laraine Newman's best character

10

continues to be Connie Conehead. Bob Newman's
best birthday present for both my ex-wives
continues to be little green Micks army knives.

Alfred E. Newman's funniest pastiche continues
to be B. B. Yeltsin. Adrian Piper walks the streets
of London with WET PAINT printed on her blouse.

My fiancée Linda Krajacik lathers herself
front and rear, singing to herself about nothing
in melodic perfecto contralto. She scrubs

her flushed face with a washcloth, then loofahs
her abs, pecs, and sternum. She scrubs and shaves
and daydreams and sings. She shampoos her hair,

rinses it, turns off the water. When she pulls back
the translucent shower curtain, a couple of scraggly
dudes in Cuervo bandannas are waiting for her

11

in the bathroom. One dude hands her a towel.
The second dude presses the well-oiled muzzle
of an Ingram MAC-10 against her pink gums

and tells her to put up her hands. "You are under
arrest!" he shouts in immaculate English. "For
what?" demands Linda, raising one hand and turning

her face from the muzzle. "For the murder of Jose
Guillermo García, Celia de la Serna, Lorenzo
Somoza, Manuel Noriega, Señor David Hidalgo,

Pilar Ternera, Roque Dalton García, Vasco 'Duende'
Gonçalves, Carmine Sandino, Santino Corleone,
a-and Jose Rodolfo Viera," says the dude with the gun.

"A-and so put down that towel already, you feelthy
leetle *desaparecida.*" Brief pause. "But Dalton García
is already dead," counters Linda. "I'm clean." The

12

scragglier dude, the one with the gun, says, "We know that."
Linda is dripping provocatively, goose bumps have risen
on cue, and she shivers. Both hands are raised, the white

towel lies on the floor. The dude who originally
gave her the towel now slaps her across the face,
twice, first with the back of his hand, then with

the front, very hard. "We already, know that!"
he says. Two nights later, at Randolph Street
Gallery, Linda stands on a table in green

suede high heels about two feet apart and pees
into a teacup: a few drops at first, then
a clear steady stream that lasts twelve,

fifteen seconds. Not a drop hits the table.
Applause. Wearing a Fearnley tartan kilt,
a Harris tweed jacket and knee socks, I pretend

13

to sternly interrogate her after she pees.
"Quite bloody finished?" I ask. "I'm pregnant,
I think," Linda says. "Not by you."

"But that sounds but medium true."
"Shakespeare?" she asks. I shake my head no.
"But speaking of the Bard of Avon,

what's the dirtiest line, by far, ever spoken
on a prime-time network situation comedy?"
She pauses, pretending to think. "Ward,"

says finally, "weren't you a little hard on
the Beaver last night?" I say, "Gee, that's correct,"
and act real astonished. "Okay, Cheez Whiz,"

she says, "tell me this. How many Irishmen
does it take to screw in a light bulb? None.
It's too fookin' hot in there. (Jaysus, you're

14

dim.) How many feminists does it take
to screw in a light bulb? That's not funny!
What do you call a Polack in a hundred-

dollar hat?" I look dim, pretend not to know.
"Well?" she says, crossing her sinewy, jewelry-
free arms. I continue to pretend not to know.

"Pope," she pronounces succinctly. Not good.
Denim-clad Catholic youths prick up their ears.
Thumbs-forward hands on her hips, Linda stands

on the table, clad in saucy green smock and high
heels, having, now mind you, already bloody peed
into a chalicelike teacup—oh Jaysus!—and down-

loaded blasphemous info through pink bee-stung
lips, unmarried and seven weeks pregnant.
"And how are women like dogshit?!" she snarls

15

à la Vlad the Impaler. I wonder. "The older they get
the easier they are to pick up!" I am stunned.
Since this noxious brand of macho naïveté and

viciousness surely isn't part of our script, I
demand to know, "Isn't that the sort of unfunny
'bad joke' that could set feminism back a couple

three weeks?" "Yo, tell me about it, Mr. Premature
Ejaculation," she snaps, whapping a palm with a fist.
"Now don't get your panties in a wad," I suggest.

Linda ignores this advice, whapping the palm even
harder. She can sense, like a dog, that I'm scared.
"What do fifteen battered husbands have in common?"

I cower and mumble, "Dunno," 'cause I don't. She milks
my uncertainty for all that it's worth, then barks
up my nostrils, "They Just Wouldn't Fuckin' Listen!"

16

Just wouldn't fuckin' listen is right. When our son
was born seven months later, we named him Jacques Moran
after the Jacques *père et fils* in Book II of the Beckett

Tetralogy, as well as after Linda's great-grandfather
Jim, who was also an artist (he whittled and stained
things), but lately we've ended up calling him Air

Jake or Buzz or just Jacques. He seems to be getting used
to having such a famous artist for a mother and all
since he spits up and cries less and less when she uses him

in her performances or we take him to see other people's.
Not that we'd ever consider leaving him home by himself
after what happened that time to QT. I mean

are you kidding? We've even added a "love of the game"
clause to his contract, which he's the only guy in the family
to have such a clause so far as I know, at least so far.

I was running scared on Zion Beach. It was ninety and hazy, real August stroke weather, so I shouldn't've been out there to begin with. I should've been out on the golf course, in fact, or back in the shade of my yard on the hammock—or at least on the range hitting balls. But I wasn't. I was out on the beach in the sun, by myself, doing what I was supposed to.

The pouches of flab on my hips swung and shook as I jogged through the pebbly sand. I turned thirty-nine back in March, and Ben Wu, my internist, has convinced me that if I don't break a pretty good sweat at least four times a week, I might not make fifty—or forty. Golf wasn't going to cut it, even if I threw in the occasional sit-up or push-up. My Achilles and shinsplints were killing me, too, and I had almost no wind at all. And when had my chest become breasts? It wasn't that easy to cover these things in the summer.

After running for ten, fifteen minutes I spotted a pair of young women leaving the water maybe eighty-five yards up ahead—a sand wedge away at the most, if I wasn't already *in* sand. Slate blue Lake Michigan waves swelled against their suits then seesawed across their legs. The shorter of the two had fine, slicked-back hair that looked like a bronze Trojan helmet. She was wearing a black one-piece suit which revealed that her shoulders and torso were lean but convex. She was something. Each step she took toward the beach reduced the hypotenuse between us and lowered the level of water around her. I slowed down a little—I couldn't slow down too much further without actually stopping—to keep her on view a bit longer.

She was nodding at something her friend said, and the friend nodded back. Waves slapped her knees as she tilted her shoulders and tugged on the back of the suit. As I said, she was something. But I kept facing north, straight ahead, so it wouldn't seem like I was gawking.

There were suddenly giggles and shrieks. "Hi, Mr. McQuethy!" and "Yo!" Oh Lord, I thought, cringing. It was Linda Wisniewski and Katie Krajacik, wading through ankle-deep water. Katie played center field on my daughter Mairead's fast-pitch softball team. Linda, who was tall and left-handed, played first. It was two of the great Zion Zephyrs! My wife and I had been rooting them on from the stands since the middle of June, watching the team go 17–5 (three of the losses had been by one run), but I hadn't recognized them without their scarlet thunderbolt "Z" caps and baggy white polyester uniforms. They were thirteen or fourteen years old. Katie had tripled to the opposite field the last game we'd been to, driving in Mairead and another girl, then torn through a stop sign by the third-base coach and been thrown out at the plate by twenty-five feet. She was the one I'd been looking at.

I stopped. "Hi, Linda. Hi, Katie." I held in my stomach and lowered my voice. "How's the water?"

"Jammin'," said Katie. She did a brief jig in the surf, then stood very still.

"Really great," Linda said.

Linda was strawberry blond with pale, freckled skin, and was wearing an orange and yellow striped suit. She was almost six foot, lanky and gaunt like a boy. Katie was tanner and denser, with precipitous cheekbones and bottle-green eyes. Her eyelids curved outward like lazy, mascaraless sine waves, the kind you might see on a Mesopotamian urn.

"Decent," they said, simultaneously.

Both of them wriggled and dripped as they gingerly stepped through the pebbles.

"Un*fun*!" Linda winced.

"Ow-ow-ow-*ow*!" Katie cried, doing her jig step again. I'd seen Mairead doing the same little jig, and I knew it was meant as a signal or joke of some sort—something to do with the Zephyrs, I guessed, but who knew. I considered offering Katie—offering either or both of them—my hand, of assisting them through the sharp pebbles, but before I could decide what to do they were standing in the sand between me and the lake. Katie hiccuped and looked at her watch. Linda sneezed.

"Bless you," I said. I tried not to look at their bodies.

"Thanks," Linda said.

"Jogging them pounds off?" asked Katie.

"Trying to, I guess," I admitted. I was shocked that she'd bring up my weight. "Trying to jog a few tons off."

None of us said anything, or even looked at each other, for eight or ten seconds. I fingered some sweat off my forehead. A gull glided by, very low, tilting its bill toward the lake.

"Where's Mairead?" Katie asked me. She shivered and hugged herself, shifting her weight from one pink wet foot to the other. Her knees were light brown and glinted with tiny gold hairs, beads of water. Green veins stood out on her wrists and the backs of her hands. She glanced at me two or three times, squinting against the low sun. I stared past her head toward Wisconsin.

"At the Gap with Felicia, I think."

"Like, that's where *we* were supposed to be going," they said, as a question almost, in sync to the pause and the syllable. It sounded as though they'd rehearsed it.

My pulse had slowed down, but I hadn't stopped sweating. I barely had caught back my breath, and my hair was a stringy, wet tangle. I didn't know what to say next. I couldn't help wonder: why *hadn't* they gone to the Gap?

A blurred image suddenly came to me: Katie in socks and a T-shirt standing outside our hall bathroom. I must have run into her during one of Mairead's giant slumber parties—probably the one for her birthday, the Saturday after Thanksgiving—but I couldn't remember exactly.

"We almost didn't recognize you without your, you know, red pants," Linda said.

"My red pants?"

"Huh?" Katie said, to her friend. They looked at each other. "Oh, gotcha. Them plaid jobs."

I nodded and shrugged. They were referring to the pair of red tartan golf slacks I'd picked up that spring in Ballybunion, and that I'd apparently worn to a couple of Zephyr games, too. I wanted to tell them that Ian Woosnam had won the damn Masters while wearing the same pair of slacks.

"They're famous," said Linda, doing her best not to smirk.

"And it's well that they should be," I told her.

A small wave broke over their feet. Katie kicked surf onto Linda, then bent down and splashed her. Linda cursed, which surprised me, then dashed back to catch what was left of the wave, trying to retaliate. Katie screamed and took off up the beach, then stopped, wheeled around. She was still in the mood for a fight.

"Azerbaijanis," called Linda.

"Not bad," called Katie. "Az yers."

"Are you still going shopping?" I asked.

They ignored me. Linda was already back in the lake, on her

knees, cupped hand cocked low in the water. Katie had raised up her arms and reared back, whinnying like a spooked stallion. I shuffled my feet in the sand, running in place with my fists near my hips, as I watched Katie edge toward the water.

"Don't be a yutz," Linda said.

"Don't *me* be a yutz?"

"And don't get your panties in a wad."

"Don't you worry."

It was the first time I'd gone running without a T-shirt, and I wished I were wearing one now.

"Don't be an eejit like Will's what I *should* say," said Katie.

"Would you shut up!"

"Who's gonna make me?"

"You're looking at her, girlfriend," said Linda, though it didn't look like she could take her. "You're looking right at her."

"Okay . . ."

I couldn't tell who would attack. Katie bashed air-guitar chords in the water, singing some song I didn't recognize in a screechy falsetto. Linda was taunting her, egging her on, imitating the way she had whinnied. I filled up my lungs and ran harder.

"Now, girls," I said, puffing and huffing.

"You ready for *this* here stuff, girlfriend?" said Linda. She threw her blond head back and whinnied.

Katie let both of her hands dangle down in the water, swinging them crosswise behind then in front of each other while weaving her knees back and forth.

"*Bawk,* buck-buck-buck . . ."

I was already sweating again, short of breath. But hadn't they heard me? And couldn't they see I was watching them? I was no more than ten feet away.

"Come on, you worthless cheeseball," said Linda, feinting a right-handed splash.

"Buck-buck-buck."

They crouched in the surf as they circled each other, squawking and clucking like chickens, on guard.

I kept running.

three

O powerful western fallen star!
O shades of night—

—WALT WHITMAN

GREAT AMERICA

1

On the evening of January 19, 1991, seventy-five
hours into Operation Desert Storm, four bands I know of
played "Purple Haze": Shrimp Boat at Metro; the Kronos
      Quartet
at Park West; violinist Nigel Kennedy, while conducting the St.
Paul Chamber Orchestra, between the Fall and Winter
      movements
of *The Four Seasons;* and Sting, as both host and musical guest
of *Saturday Night Live.* Another six dozen ensembles, in concert
halls, studios, garages, or stadia may have covered it sometime
that evening, but no one keeps very close track of these things
anymore. In any event, the invocations of Hendrix's spirit
were welcome gestures of reproach as the Cubist F-117's
and Futurist Tomahawks went about their grim business, even
when we reminded ourselves that it was the well-oiled jihad
machinery of an undereducated dipshit like Saddam Hussein
they were obliterating, not Ho Chi Minh's barefoot minions.

Throughout the evening NBC news briefs showed Tel
Aviv bracing for Scud attacks, F-15's taking off
from huge carriers, and the president speaking with cool
determination and sounding remarkably like Dana Carvey.
"Weekend Update" included a skit in which a Tomahawk
      missile
made a direct hit on a reporter in Baghdad—in homage, perhaps,
to the opening scene of *Gravity's Rainbow,* in which Pirate
      Prentice
imagines himself being nailed in the skull by the tip of a German
V-2. Then again, perhaps not. By this point Der Stinglehoffer

had already played "Mad About You," the latest hit single
in his ongoing McCartneyization, and appeared in four
skits, including one as an arch combination of 'Enry 'Iggins
and Victor Frankenstein, another as an awkward college boy
struggling to introduce his loony fiancée to his parents. But why
did he (and Shrimp Boat and Kronos and Kennedy) play "Purple
        Haze"?

(My daughter and wife would happily, both of them, kill
to be able to ask him.) The song's a succinct acid blues
with an adequate rhythm section, spacey but straightforward
enough lyrics, and a jagged, incendiary guitar line.
It apparently functions just as well as NutraSweet jingle
or all-purpose garage-band fodder as it does as "arrangement
for three pianos" for the out-there ensemble Ensemble.
But its connotative power as a sometime anti-war anthem
has mainly to do with its emergence during the summer
of 1967, on millions of record players and hundreds
of millions of radios from Selma to Da Nang, Port Huron
to London, and Paris to Saigon as the baddest, catchiest licks
on the soundtrack to "Vietnam," i.e., to the roiling matrix
of dope, civil rights, rock and roll, loud clothes, large
hair, the war in Southeast Asia, and the protests of same

in cities, politburos, and on campuses all over the planet
—just as Herman Hupfeld's "As Time Goes By," a haunting
but thoroughly apolitical love song, has become ineluctably
associated with *la Résistance,* "Stayin' Alive" can't help makin'
you think of Betty and Ger, or Mozart's G minor quintet
will remind you you're going to die but won't make it seem

all that terrible. Hardly. The fact is, we've come
in the last quarter century to read Jimi Hendrix
as a braid-weaving common denominator: simultaneously
Western, African, and Native American; urban and cosmic,
subversive and patriotic, combative and peaceloving;
bluesy, metallic, serious, pop, avant garde. His music
took mindbending, uncorporate risks—and paid off.
His swagger and verve, with and without his guitar,
constituted an unignorable affront to the corporate

mentality then emerging as the pop music industry
began to achieve blue-chip-scale profitability,
and, as expected, he paid for that attitude big-time:
humiliating royalty percentages, circumscribed airplay
on black *and* white radio stations, getting relentlessly
hassled to buy into some well nigh extravagantly racist
and or naively pacifist rhetorics . . . plus we let the guy die
far from home, in the megalopolis, London, that launched
and revered him, by suffocating on his own vomit. However.
To the extent that all wars tend to be organized and supported
by unbent, religio-corporate interests, any song he recorded
still can effectively stand as a shorthand gesture of reproach:
thumbs down, a raised middle finger, a peace sign. Because even
in a comparatively lyrics-intensive ditty like "Purple Haze"
Jimi, true to his words, let his fingers do most of the talking.

2

A windsurfer whose name I never catch escapes Havana
and celebrates the Fourth on TV in Miami
with a Michelob Dry in one hand, a

brunette in the other. A second, my
second wife's boss, Jana Wright,
drifts serenely toward the dunes of northwest Indiana
just as Dale Kim is losing a leg to a great
white a quarter mile off San Clemente, California.
Peter Brown, Jana's husband, wings Jana's keel
showing off for *his* boss, Tony Jones. Meantime Moira Ni
Chuilleannain and Maire Mhac an tSaoi's feet get badly stung
twice by white men-of-war within sight of Nantucket,
but they do get themselves safely blown
back to Chappaquiddick.

3

Tens of thousands of highways and avenues, lanes,
tunnels, cars, parks, aircraft carriers, towing
services, rivers, insurance underwriters, children,

centers for the performing arts, golf courses, cities,
trusts, technical colleges, and savings and loans
have been named after Abraham Lincoln, and he graces

our five-dollar bill: the notorious bearded-but-
mustacheless visage; on the back, his then new white
marble Memorial. That Illinois is the Land of Lincoln

is proclaimed on eight million pairs of license plates
above such mottoes as T BILLS, JE VENDS, INSR LAW, KNUK
L HD, XTRVRT, MR PIP 33, MS WHIZ, BRUUUCE, and the like.

In Ed Paschke's hairy portrait, reproduced on the cover
of *TriQuarterly 52* by then editor Jonathan Brent, Mr.
Lincoln emerges from bands of cyans and blues, bloody

scarlets, a shimmering vertical-hold problem tattooed
with faint neon doodles, looking dapper but schizoid,
plugged-in, his modern tie's knot a neat four-in-hand;

the back of the issue featured Paschke's *Purple Ritual,*
an earlier ('68) portrait of Lee Harvey Oswald
hefting his mail-order rifle, surrounded by shield-

clutching eagles, purple haze, and stars-and-stripes bunting.
On Mount Rushmore Lincoln's craggy features barely emerge
from the found cubist planes in the granite, more still

a part of the mountain, certainly, than thin-lipped,
commanding George Washington, whose entire head,
chest, and left shoulder are rendered, and even

whose lapels and cravat Gutzon Borglum (whose mountain-
carving ambitions were sparked by the Daughters
of the Confederacy) has sculpted in subtle detail.

In Borglum's early maquette Lincoln was peeking
around Thomas Jefferson, a third of his face
obscured by the talented Federalist's sidelock

till a fault in the rock forced a rethink:
Lincoln was given his own wall of granite,
perpendicular to Theodore Roosevelt, Borglum's late

hero; four-story pine trees now thrive in the rubble
which fell as Abe's face was revealed, as an afterthought
almost, by the chisels and sanders and dynamite.

Robert Frank's deadpan photograph *Bar—Detroit,* a kind
of ironic half-Rushmore, captures framed reproductions
of paintings of Washington and Lincoln suspended

from a ceiling above a YOU MUST BE 21 AND PROVE IT
notice and a plastic largemouth bass, and separated
by a glowing and windblown (the a.c.?) American flag.

In the cracked plate of Alexander Gardner's final
photographic portrait, taken barely two weeks
before Ford's Theatre, Lincoln's exhausted,

determined features—caved-in sockets, grim sense
of humor intact—emerge between the planes inhabited
by his oversized earlobe and crooked bow tie

into grim, wrinkled focus, the diagonal crack
in the plate fairly scalping him, suggesting both neatly
jigsawed pieces of a too-easy puzzle, and cutting

him off close to the point where Booth's bullet
entered his skull. Gardner by then had discarded
the plate, assuming he could always make others.

Lincoln is also the street running east and west
at the north end of Evanston I religiously take
on my bike from our house to the lake every evening.

4

nd was that, at the turn of the
millennium, its matrix of democratic, cultural, economic, and
military institutions, albeit imperfect, were still the most thoroughly
developed on the planet. To live in that temperate nation was to ma

5

Former Ball-Mart clerk Kathleen Braker testified Tuesday
to having sold a Nolan Ryan rookie card to Bryan Wrzesinski

for twelve dollars. The Lucite-encased trading card was marked
        "1200,"
but Ms. Braker couldn't recall whether the number

contained a comma, decimal, or dollar sign. (*Beckett
Baseball Card Monthly* lists a 1968

Nolan Ryan rookie card in perfect condition
at $925.) Ball-Mart owner Joe Irmen, who was not in

his store when the transaction was made, filed suit
seeking to have the card returned, or $1188

in cash. Television coverage
of the trial has been extensive, and Wrze-

sinski's blue eyes, blond crew cut, and the simple
gold chain he wears round his neck have endeared him to
        hundreds

of thousands of viewers in the Chicagoland area. But when called
	upon
to testify as to the card's present whereabouts, thirteen-year-old
	Bryan

told Joe Irmen's lawyer, "I traded it."
Judge Ann B. Jorgensen sprang from the bench

and ordered attorneys for both parties into her chambers;
ninety seconds later she returned to the bench, nearly falling after

tripping on a stair ledge, retrieved two small documents
then returned to her chambers. Fifty-six minutes later

attorneys emerged from those chambers and said that the case
had been continued until 2 p.m. Thursday. The kiss

6

Wendy Robb Chamberlain, volunteer organist
at the Channelview Missionary New Baptist

Church, tried to arrange for the murder
of her former neighbor, the former

Germantown High School Baton-Twirling Champion Wanda
Sands, in an effort to influence a cheerleading contest

involving their daughters, Shanna Sands and Chelsea Schaefer.
Ms. Chamberlain's objective was to cause Shanna emotional grief

sufficient to make her less of a threat to Chelsea
during the rigorous competition for slots on *waiting to hear the*
worst

about the daughter's grieved performance on next year's freshman
cheerleading squad at Channelview High School. The two girls
have been

close friends since second grade as well as one
another's chief rivals. (Shanna is president

Chelsea vice-president of the student council of Alison Friend
Junior High School.) Ms. Chamberlain, determined

to bring this rivalry to a decisive conclusion, asked her former
brother-in-law,
Terry Schaefer, to help her find a killer. This proved a
miscalculation.

When Mr. Schaefer informed police of her plan, a male
undercover
detective *he's so cute* was detailed to pose as a cheerleader

just kidding a killer for hire. Ms. Chamberlain, who is divorced
and unemployed, first discussed a contract for the murder

of both Shanna and her mother, but balked at the detective's
asking price of $7500. She eventually offered a pair *of fives*

over deuces of her small diamond earrings as down payment for
    the murder
of Ms. Sands only. When the detective accepted this offer and
    showed her

his badge, Ms. Chamberlain shook her head *so like candy* The day
after the indictment was issued, as Shanna and Chelsea

were being inducted into the school's honor society, the alphabet
dictated they stand onstage beside one another. "Both mamas

were present as if nothing had happened at all,"
said James Barker, the principal. "Nobody made a fuss."

He went on to inform this reporter that two years earlier
Ms. Chamberlain had tried unsuccessfully to get Shanna
    disqualified from *the other side of summer*

a cheerleading competition by invoking a technicality in the rules
(no snapping gum during punts). Last year, he said, she showed
    up at school

on the day students were voting on cheerleader candidates and
    handed out rulers
and pencils bearing the slogan CHELSEA SCHAEFER CHEERLEADER.

As a result, Chelsea was disqualified. Professional coaches
were subsequently hired to help prepare Chelsea for this

year's competition, but the deadline for entries, he said,
just happened to fall on the morning her mother was arrested.

7

Showers by candlelight, six-irons
into a lightning storm at sunset
over the Badlands, then back into Wall
just in time for Ruddock and Tyson

The Rematch. . . . *Coy*otes. *Coy*otes.
Is this a great country
or what. (But a 3-Peat?
Bull*shit*!) The hardest states to get

in the License Plate Game are Lou-
isiana, Alaska, Rhode Island, New
Hampshire, and, of course, Hawaii,
although Moira conveniently

spotted one as we exited Think, North
Dakota, but this got ruled (3–1) a
Totally Unconfirmed Sighting, Sucker
(yielding the acronym for Isiah

"Hey, I still like our chances" Thomas's
other nickname). At least she appreciates beauty: the weather
arranging itself around canyons and glaciers, across
Kintla Lake, Logan Pass, and St. Mary, our

bug-spattered two-car caravan cruising Going-
to-the-Sun: the Lynches' '67
Corvette, chrome-rust-and-silver on silver,
dual quads, the 427;

our red and black Honda in honor
of Good News and Scottie, Mr. Bill,
Will the Thrill, PJ and BJ and Pax,
Money, Sheikh, Horace, et al.,

then north up to Swiftcurrent Lake with the moonlight
on velvet-antlered moose and, finally, our TVless suite
at Many Glacier Hotel to make *in*decent, shivering
love, windows wide open, in the cold of late June.

8

Arkansas pony knees steal while stampeding
33 on a run-out and later
swiping at playing exceptional tennis lysergic and licking

a Blow Pop a badass Masai only
swiping at playing occasional Tetras ly
sucking a Blow
Pop acid a Tootsie

Pop tee off the *uh-oh* her purple the dogleg his nightstick
then eagles the tightest par 5 down at Endsville on Jell-O viola
a C-scroll of blotter a cello bandanna

harbodica indium fiddle some migraine from Lodi
fiddle photographer must've assumed Cinerama
Fiddle depends on a regular 7π
racquet so much to a

girl on a red and black
Trek 33 not a cognate
but chickens that black chick beside the big Czech

dude in the corner the lame
beer dose equivalent drinking
and driving consider
this to spin Pop *this* orange

sunshine this purple roadtrip her Honda
consider this skinpop a sidetrip eugenic to slow strip a goner
on Demerol *Grosse*

no not generic no *Fuge*
you know the cuddly that hetero bumper
crop all this fugal procedure Madonna
in scudly transition

trax *i*-receipt from the oscillatory First in C yo
ional Bank o
f minor

Wilmette's broad lawns and medium minds to which *I owe*
I owe it's off to work I go in a
black-and-white landscape with lush grainy gray values no
starkplush Sternfeldian Ektachrome burbscape yeah *sí* the

medium two-shot to knock down the eighteen-foot jumper
knock down the flat house on Hunter
918 isn't no majors no skiers in April the lengths

I'll go to the distance
in your eyes not a
quasidyslexic did Arra non 69 meantime Moira
Ni Chuilleannain and Maire Mhac an tSaoi's

legs get badly stung twice by the white
men-of-war within sight of Nantucket
but they do get themselves safely blown
back to Chappaquiddick Island's very own

Go now my sons
in Rose's hazel and trembling voice
and make 13 ejaculations

properly cross no the Little
Wilma go cross Mrs. Robinson no make that President
        Robinson
section crosstown go traffic Pall Mall across African
cross out September October until

Novemberless triple sec Fred-Fred
the Freddy November the *Pamela* isn't at Dorothy's
Fred Hickman's electric piano how stoned

is Freddy not very as Declan's old Jazzmaster North
America two Hamlet nil
linco parka phylo rre riseth
Dude Friday's 28 points 9 assists 14 boards versus Hendrix

College no way he's that frank he must bother
those pounds off no $380 play-off seat Jim not back of the *organ*
he can I guess always print others

great Birnbaum pacific
rim this dude his prune juice reply
card raises the ante okay Homes the replay
pronounce it he rimmed them's terrific

great date with his secretary's yeah this is dynamite ham
a great blank in ¾ time she's
an excellent driver Jim Durham's

making it talk so why don't we hire him back
he describes it so great he's just ripped Great
America great golfing great ankles eat
Casement no Southey no Coleridge

StairMaster StairMaster
on down the road no
seconds on pasta no pie à la mode

StairMaster StairMaster
climbing to heaven
those Jimmy Page riffs
give me just the right leaven

not smoking
not smoking
not smoking

Splashwater Falls the Shock
Wave the Shooting Gallery
rhythmic percussion is African melody
more European this dismal cock

galvanizing ritual just because Peewee was framed
grab some binch because actually *kiss*
but I tend to prefer bigender encounters myself this

from the long and absurdly ambitious
poem entitled *Nebraska* by J. L. McQuist
The whole place is pretty monotonous
unless you're The Boss or a botanist

9

My love, thy hair
is one kingdom.
Now take off your
clothes or I'll have my uncle drive you home.

Pushed Leon Overboard.
Soon Own New York.
But not Baghdad. By Filius Fibonacci, who'd rediscovered
pizza by 1492, we shall attack.

Two Ethiopian women. . . . But this other dude was like
"So you've swept me back down
into Hades, I who could've walked
with live souls above the earth, who'd've slept

among the flowers
at last." Would he now gather turds
for his grandmother's garden? . . . We thought not. His Tower's
Chicago: nine bundled structural tubes for big shoulders, Third

City, workplace of Puckhead and Money and Pudge, Gloomy Gus
and Dick Daley, fierce as a dog with its tongue
lappin' for action, Home, cunnilingus
with a human footprint, snufflin' down into the mung . . .

Later, the 49-year-old AIDS patient admitted
he and his co-workers had sought out and beaten
gay men in the Greater Chicagoland Area between
1982 and 1988. "In the neighborhood

of several times a week," he told doctors. "Too many
times to remember." He often got cuts on his knuckles
and large amounts of victims' blood on his hands.
Doctors reported the former truck driver "chuckled"

when informed he had probably brought the disease
on himself. "Then he grunted and shook his head."
His wife did not become infected with the virus
because he'd been impotent for over a decade.

So no more of this Romeo Sadface, okay
Uncle Sam?
Americans don't read too much poetry.
Dipshits seem

to prefer the company of a foot
and a half of tinted split ends
stapled to the top of a skeleton
who'd cash in her family for a piece of ass:

Stanley and Iris Traumatize the Daughter
Stanley and Iris Deconstruct the B-flat Major Quartet
Stanley and Iris Start Their Own Art School
Stanley and Iris Get Pregnant

The thing is, we want to be stars
in America, and millions of us are,
although as Professor Richard S. Wrong has demon-
strated, eighty-seven percent of our women

and seventy-three percent of our men believe
in a heaven or hell. (While eighty-one
percent of both genders believe they have
good to excellent chances of going to heaven, Wrong

reminds us that less than four percent think they've got similar
        chances
of going to hell.) Dads sometimes die. Moms hire hit men,
        electioneer
shamelessly to help daughters not to lose
cheerleading contests. (Everyone swears

they got hacked in the act, but Stripe isn't buying it.) Boys
        commit acts of extortion
then plagiarize themselves in order to control the trading rights
        to Nolan
Ryan's rookie card. Girls sell the card for twelve dollars. Yet
        even at Woodstock we stand for
the national anthem. We love it. And Robert De Niro? Jane
        Fonda? Get back here

this instant, you pair of ass-miserable puckheads! . . . That's
        better.
Word up. We forgive you. (We *do*.) Your hair is one kingdom,
all that, but show us those Nautilized abs (just for starters)
or we'll have our uncle drive you home.

10

Stamina. Game
Boy. Comanche
(no Mohawks).
Foolishly running
on empty. Okay.
Wall Drug. The Badlands.
Pierre. No Rhode
Island plate yet.
Okay. An Alaska.
82. 70.
9. Devils Tower.
Prince of Wales. Cedar
Butte. Illinois.
United States

90. If Tetras
the Devil
danced in empty pockets
he'd have a ball in mine.

11

MONTANA POET-PHYSICIAN-PROFESSOR, 45, attractive, never-married woman seeks spiritually evolved, financially secure man for whitewater rafting, marriage and children. Photo a must. PO Box 1228, St. Mary MT 59434-1228.

GIVING, ADVENTURE-LOVING, FRANCOphile, youthful, attractive, much loved widower, NYC professional, 63, with strong interest in my work, nature, the arts, intellectual issues, seeks tender man with breadth of intellect, successful in his career, of good character, to love in a committed relationship. NYR Box 1951.

SLIM, FLEXIBLE, JBWM, 48, SEEKS lady who expects her every wish to be carried out. PO Box 666, Waterbury CT 06720.

EUROPEAN-BORN DNRJM SEEKS COLLABORATIVE lover. Exhibiting artist, slim, handsome, athletic, 40s, financially secure, seeks very bright, easy-going, pretty SWF into exercise to work together on mutually conceived projects, articles, books and to share arts, travel and commitment. NYR Box 1979.

NYMPHOLEPTIC WIDOW: I'VE GOT LOOKS, brains, health, sweetness, and a passion for music, travel, the outdoors, life. Is an unencumbered, stable, intellectually developed, lovable man (48–60) an unattainable goal? Reader Box 8817.

NYC WRITER/TEACHER, 57, 5'8", independently wealthy, seeks best friend/lover to share classical music, films, poetry (Paz, Beckett, Rich, Parson), good conversation, outdoors and ??? NYR Box 1875.

SOCIALLY OUTRAGED? NONDOCTRINAIRE? Slim, eye-catching, highly imaginative, ticklish DIVORCEE, 40s, is happiest with a tall, honorable, unusual, cerebral (musical? artistic?) soulmate. Exchange photos? Box 817, Minneapolis MN 55401.

TERRIFIC WOMAN, PETITE, EBULLIENT, 50, delighted, a poet and lover of the arts, seeks terrific, delighted, financially secure woman 23–55 for friendship and love ASAP. Photo a plus. DDS Box 227.

NEEDS A DIRTY GIRL. SBM, 35, in Pacific Heights seeks a cute white girl, 18–24, with a shaved pussy for safe sex and spankings in a sweaty sauna. Call it a job or call it a date, but earn money now while you masturbate. TeleClub Ext. 27905.

NEOPHYTE THRALL SEEKS SUPERIOR FEMALE. SWM, 29, funny, educated, healthy, inexperienced. Fresh material to be shaped as you see fit, trained to obey all of your needs: S/M, B/D, foot/body massage, cooking/cleaning. TeleClub Ext. 21725.

CONSIDER THE ALTERNATIVES. I'm a bi-F, 33, tall, curva-ceous, and playful. He is 33, shy, and thoughtful. Both HIV − . If you can imagine a life lived in balance as a life lived as three, then R.S.V.P. TeleClub Ext. 27213.

GODDAMN THE SUN. Nocturnal young gothster seeks those of
like mind for friendship and/or "romance." Me: tall, slim, athletic,
bi-WM, UCB undergraduate. Into Thelema and runes. Love Berg-
man, Nortons, Mausers, and Poe. We'll ride. TeleClub Ext. 27169.

12

Bring all your money when you come
to Great America. Entire
sunburned families do. Single moms
and dads with their kids for

the weekend, visitation rights
for perhaps all of August;

grammar school girls with one strap
of their overalls dangling down
to their coltish and intricate kneecaps;

sneering, tattooed, earringed teenagers
with minuscule pimples and mustaches,
real jerkoffs, in heavy metal polyester
T-shirts: Anthrax, Motorhead, U.S.,

G 'N' R, Husker Du, Poison, the same bad Rod
Stewart–Farah Fawcett hairdo
to a man as their fidgety dates; clearly proud

devotees of Rich Falk Basketball Camp and Zora Neale
Hurston, the White Sox, The Pogues, Jane's Addiction; the usual

well-behaved, plainly groomed and clothed Asians . . .

Suddenly this gorgeous, unmated
Latina in one-ply white Dago
T with the dewy, finely delineated
backs of her knees revealed under slow

grind and spark of blue skirt
comes lowriding by *and then gone!*
as we're herded through tubular aluminum mazes in tight
longitudinal zigzag, penned in

36 rows going one way
37 rows in the other

configured in–
geniously so that one

only rarely simply
stands there and waits, every

last person in their fleshly summer glory: no-tan
lines, cellulite, weightlifter triceps and squints, armpit hair,
         noshing

cheesedogs, powder blue cotton candy, burritos, icecream
novelties, Pizza Luigi, soft pretzels, all of us trudging along

for fifty-five minutes for sixty or seventy seconds
on Splashwater Falls, Ameri-Go-Round, Rolling Thunder, the
         Demon . . .

In line for the Eagle I spot Samuel Beckett's gulls'
eyes glaring out from the chest of a slackly buxom Ms.

I'm im-
pressed. Because upon snatching a brief *hmm*

surreptitious but closer inspection, it's the Sucking Stones
passage from the Tetralogy *distributed them equally between*

my four
above her poor

breasts. The front side of one
leg of her kneelength shorts is red. The front

of the other leg's black and features a furrow-browed
snorting red bull with white red-tipped horns. The pattern's
        reversed

on the back of the shorts, except there's no logo to break up the
        line
of her backside, *de dum* . . . The American

Eagle's an old-fashioned wooden double roller coaster,
an abstract white boa constrictor at its lunatic leisure

reminiscent of Riverview, the El, or even the
Polo Grounds and earlier stadia,

all wood, nails and screws,
latticed gridwork and primitive buttresses,

its superstructure the crack of
a bullwhip, the wave

of a virtual lariat. Not too unGuggenheimlike,
either. Painted white—site specific,

I guess. We ride it, burritos
engorge our esophagi, my balls, in the throes

of a series of too sudden de- and then re-escalations, vibrate and
      rise not
unpleasantly, then we climb out and stagger for root

beer at A Stand Without A Name, saving the Shock Wave for
      last, woozy
but still on the lookout for saucy

tan kneecaps, that profile . . . In the meantime The Amazing
Alfredeux guesses weights, ages, months of birth and gives special
      prizes.

At the Moosejaw Trading Post can be purchased genuine
      woodcraft items,
wind chimes, pottery, no moosejaws at all but still most of the
      items

you'd expect to discover at An Old-Time Trading Post, while
      The Plush Pony's
a menagerie, of course, of the latest soft and cuddly stuffed
      animals . . .

Unearthing the Shock Wave, what will archaeologists make
of two thousand six hundred feet of steel track

with charred, bubbled chips of Dodger blue paint nuked into
        neat, twisted
loops—some sort of super short, unrapid

transit system for narrow (solar?) cars apparently not
going anyplace terrifically

interesting? These days it slowly climbs 170 feet
up a very steep track, jerkily, nerve-racking, clackety *shit*

now there's no turning back as it silently screams into a twelve-story
        dive at 62 mph
then banks immediately into the first of *you're going to retch*

of the seven, count 'em, inside
out loops inside

of which it *really* starts to jerk you around: upside down,
backward, G-forces whipping you sideways. You turn maybe
        fifteen

degrees to glance at your son and a twist snaps your head back
        around.
Your elbow gets banged. You feel giddy and scared, and you
        understand

clearly that *I think I'm gonna hurl*
the Shock Wave is Great

America's intensest roller coaster. It is not
a close call. When it stops

and the smiling 15-year-old attendant unlocks your safety *fun?*
bar, you climb out but can't hardly walk. Your kids, of course,
      both can

and do, way ahead. You, eventually, manage. To, sort of, walk.
      To see, in the unruly lines hurriedly doubling
back for more, that other folks, too, look shook, glazed and
      happy. They're ready.

13

Ming McMichael, when asked on camera by this reporter
whether the current Bears' defensive front four

might be getting too old, admitted he had
seen some blood

on the toilet paper
that morning, but added it had pr-

obably come from his wife
Deborah's fingernail,

then reminded me that the Bears
were, once again, 1–0. . . .

Prince's butt this reporter
would rather not get into.

14

Although opportunities
for fraud (see section *blah*
blah blah of Ohio's new criminal code) seem
not all that unlikely

we've settled for letting
our T-shirts proclaim where
we've been or what lately we pledge
our allegiance to, e.g., Air

Pippens, Mozart's two-hundredth deathday, Beautiful Butte,
23, Miniature, Joyce, X, Duende, *The Paris Review,*
R.E.M., Just Another Band From L.A., the Sucking Stones
passage from the Tetralogy, the Hard Rock Cafe in Quxu.

15

This year's Independence Day fireworks in Think,
North Dakota, feature aromas of hairspray, freshly
mown lawns and, after a while, clouds of pink
gunpowder drifting out over the trailers, and after
a little while longer, sparkling green Iraqi
and blue UN tanks facing off. "Mama, look," drawls
a little blond boy as reports rocket back
from the foothills. "Great big tanks," yells
his mama, pointing them out. "Go ka*boom*."

16

Ya won.

Mot sucks
iron *anos*

raw and a

dada
DNA

war's on. A

no–risk
custom?

No way.

17

Exterior. Montana Route 332. Day.

A red and black Honda Accord moves west at 85 mph along the two-lane highway. On the stereo: Elvis Costello's "Any King's Shilling."

Driver's POV down the road, through the windshield. To the right: a whitewater stretch of Tongue River. Ahead: Bighorn Mountains below a dark ridge of storm clouds.

PASSENGER (V.O.)
It *is* always the most boring member of
the band who ends up writing the book.

DRIVER (V.O.)
. . . even worse than having to listen
to your own voice on tape.

After several beats, in spite of the spectacular scenery, focus on the
windshield itself. The Tongue is a blur to the right. The passenger
hums along with Elvis Costello. Suddenly a honeybee splatters
against the windshield.

PASSENGER (V.O.)
Whoa, *dude!*

DRIVER (V.O.)
One very dead bug, on my windshield.

A jagged line of splattered honey continues to shiver and crawl up
the windshield.

PASSENGER (V.O.)
Little Bighorn River, 26 miles.

DRIVER (V.O.)
Harold Baines for Wilson Alvarez,
the Bulls and the Pistons . . .

PASSENGER (V.O.)
Custer versus Sitting Bull, a couple
three F–117's versus—   CUT TO:

18

Gros Ventre geometry. Snake.
United States 191. Jenny Lake.

Shevardnadze's condos
and ranch under young

upside down mountains
rising from lake beds in

pink and slate
light, each generation

equidistant from eternity,
says Moira. You see?

Unstable gneisses
and schists exposed by

block faulting
of course, way back when.

Something like us
I suppose.

19

On this towering wall
is to be inscribed a memorial

laid on . . . in a daze: Illinois,
Illinois, Illinois,

South Dakota through amber
waves of heat. South Dakota

Truck. Minnesota.
Illinois. North Dakota.

If the illusion is real
let them give you a ride

in their Show Me State Olds-
mobile Cutlass. I'm Proud

To Be An American. We ♥
Joseph and Mary. I Support

Our Troops In The Gulf. JEU AVE.
If He's Got Thunder Appeal

Let Him Be On Your Side.
And it says If the illusion is real

on this towering wall
is to be inscribed a memorial

laid on by the hand
of a great artist. *And*

it says Our tour renewed our sense
of patriotic pride at the wonders this great

man accomplished—Jim Karl, Marco
Island, Florida. Ohio.

Illinois. Illinois.
No Rhode Island.

20

Ever tried
Suicide?

My anorexic first wife—who's already
Been pregnant more times (6), by

The way, and by more different men
(3) than the average white trash,
Ghetto sister or schlong-shlurpin'
Loser she's always so anxious

To vomit her contempt for—now
Has, twice. Just swallowed 40 Dalmane
Then cut her right wrist *ow ow ow*
In three places. Got fierce diarrhea

And bled a lot, but recovered as planned
To love again another day. A-and

She wasn't really in sexual love
With the death of her own race
I don't think. Just wanted some

Attention: Gotta go now, kids,
Go try playing in the traffic
'Cause my best friend's name
Is Tantivy Mucker-Maffick.

21

I'M DESPERATE! NOT because I'm ugly, fat, stupid or dull (I'm none of those things). I'm a little shy and haven't met a man lately (who isn't ugly, fat, stupid or dull), but I haven't given up on meeting WS/DM, 25–46, who is intelligent, socially conscious (without being naive), sensitive, caring, fit, attractive, and, above all, fun! Mail Matchbox 40447.

REEF THE MAIN AND TRIM the jib! I'm going for a first-place finish. When I'm not racing sailboats, I finance giant real estate deals, so why did I get a degree in music? I'm a 30 yo DSWM 5'10" 195 and very good looking. If you're a petite, attractive SWF 18–29 and are (very good) looking for an honest, no-games relationship, call me. Mail Matchbox 40579.

22

Moira has to pee
as we cross the Missouri.

So does Burt, a
mile or so later.
A couple three
miles after
that, so do I.

23
I'm wearing his shoes when we meet,
the black '91 playoff models. He's manning

the second urinal over, wearing self-designed navy
blue jams above lean, veiny

thoroughbred knees, calves, and ankles.
My son's staring up past my head, so agog

he can't pee. Ditto with Dad, for the moment.
Before either of us can say anything

he turns and stares back: one tiny ear,
brown-yellow eyes, onset of scraggly goatee. Clears

his throat. Is he going to say something to us?
Can *we* speak to *him*? Shake his hand? . . .

Keeping his tongue in his cheek
(maybe he thinks I'm Chuck

Person) as he taps
off the last several drops, he tucks

himself in
and is gone.

24

Moira and I are real nervous.
We're walking up Mulberry Street
and some ripped Chinese dude lurches by
with Hendrix's "Star-Spangled Banner"
exploding from out of his boombox.
But that's not the reason we're nervous.

Because all of a sudden it happens.
We do it. We're standing there
outside of Luna, two doors from Moira's
old man's new apartment. We fiddle
with each other's fingers, then kiss.
Killerdiller. Our tongues even touch

for a second, but as soon as they do
there's this *flavor* that yanks us against
one another, makes us tilt sideways and back.
I'm like, that was really incredible.
"I gotta go in now," goes Moira, grinning a little.
"Like I really do have to go in now."

25

tape bootleg discs *mit* the hoople
loop the loop yeah this is scrutator sale Morrie Mages
this greatness it's great wouldn't scruple
one more triple double further details in *GW* pp.

23–33 kj an ucK LK and M he d arkskin Na
guage the blues bage the blues so ther d
wops are wanged after all after blue after blue

is Medbh's favorite colors the cockeyed way time
is money for lunatic leadfoot Islamic Manhattan
taxi drivers can preside blip the doo-wah the fax th men en IRS
            rhyme
lang wah a president never waves back no way man at least not
            to black men

the president wah wah he throve
on the blah blah blah President Robinson
president pre duh the president pre he presides no resides in the t

in the p in the Cage in the two-way m
watching his language the man
my mother loves mother unutterable un
loves him

but Hating the Holloway-Huxtables won wom was Thomas
            Pynchon
Laurie Anderson did Lucille Ball Nelson Fox or Denoon
in F minor though Natalie Wood for two weeks of fun and

instruction this one guy's skull's shaved
completely except for a strip
of bristle up top and the last
three-fourths of an inch

phased in perfectly of two-inch-wide mid-cheek black sideburns
and instruction this one guy's skull's shaved
completely except for a single

elongated pyramid right where his wave
would've been overlaps 23
advanced endometriosis singing so jaggedly
three point six fucking billion zaires and the Kodalux Scottie P.

S. the blotter's on Civil War photographs 137
228 then are left in the spectral irradiance fa
ember will assist in keeping the classrooms

and studios in good blanking order not wearing Shaq's
two-foot-long tube socks nor I. Reed Books underwear Lucky
        he jaggedly quacks
Sincerely yours
Chuck Person just kidding DB yo it's Scottie for

oh my God Vlade and Clyde it's the *oublieux* tarantulas *yes* 23
        after Bowie
Bird's in traction except for the games 'tis a ticklish affair oh *my*
I must say not bad for a Person Changing Hospitals

Every Night so no one would know
where she was driving
my third wife as fast
as I could to the hospital

26

unable to differentiate
anymore between 10th Street in Great

Falls and Ogden Avenue in Downers Grove: identical
K Marts and Wildlifes and Wendy's, Isuzus, Cruella de Vils

27

    rap, this to include any and all behavior, verbal
or physical, which tends to stigmatize an individual

on the basis of race, Vietnam-era veteran status, weight,
sexual orientation, marital status, skin color, height,

athletic ability, ancestry, age, eye-to-hand coordination,
creed, gender, handicap, ethnicity, or national origin.

Let no one doubt this here is a multicultural institution
that encourages applications from minorities and women.

She does, on the plus side, seem to share some of the same
epistemological anxiety we've recently in this country come

to expect from, oh, say, can you c

28

The national anthem at sunrise
August 17, 1969—summer of Manson,
Nixon's halfhearted troop withdrawal

and Neil Armstrong's walk on the moon—
on a dairy farm ten miles outside Bethel,
New York. Without words, in this context,
it takes a few bars to make out the melody
through the visceral haze of distortion,
scattering quarks and dislodged muoniums
oscillating at zero-point energy
toward 130 dB, but as soon as we do
we're locked into it. James Marshall
Hendrix, all business, has *ambushed*
the imagination of a whole generation again.
Mah felluh Amuricuns, it's . . . The Kid.
Jamestown. The Acid King. Lefty. A red
rolled bandanna bisects his these days
barely medium-sized afro, this to go
with a white buckskin Navajo surplice
and blue velvet bellbottoms: *Bone!*
in the U.S.A., he was . . . The backward
and upside down white-on-white Stratocaster
is going ballistic. No showboating dental
or behind-the-back picking. No somersaults,
muscle shirts, processed hair, spotlights,
chartreuse feather boas, or ritual lighter
fluid. No amp-humping, either, this morning.
Except for the ten-inch fringe on his sleeves
flapping like albino hawk wings, or eagles',
he may as well be standing at attention
as the notes whang and toggle, feeding back hard
through the Marshalls. He's making it talk
with a vengeance. The air cavalry's "rockets'

red glare" gets warped into painterly screeches,
onomatopoeia at Mach 1.7;
"bombs bursting in air" becomes blistering
napalm cacophony, hyperincendiary payloads
arcing down into inhabited jungle—as Beethoven
under these circumstances might have rendered
this hijacked, unwonderful hymn to Anacreon,
inventing outlandish contrapuntal alignments
and vertical tone combinations, most likely hammering
away through a Fuzz Face on a Rickenbacker twelve-string
or a Synclavier II suitably retooled by Rog Mayer. . . .
As "proof through the night that our flag was still there,"
Hendrix, deadpan, interpolates George M. Cohan's
"Over There," flashing us back to another Great War's
gung ho vigor and shrapneled, Jim-dandy
aftermaths, then continues the martial motif
on "the land of the free and the home of the brave"
by making the Strat trill like bagpipes.

Couple more reverb-charged chords and it's over.
There's nothing much, really, to say. We're agog.

We've all of us by now heard hundreds of covers
—by marching bands, pianists, Arditti and barber-

shop quartets, altos and tenors and baritones, pop
stars (Whitney Houston stooping to lip-syncing it

at Joe Robbie as flags waved and fighters screamed over
her wig, Roseanne Barr at Jack Murphy, Linda Ronstadt

at Dodger, even Wynton Marsalis going a little bit flat
in the Superdome, Mariah Carey forgetting the words

but still ripping sweetly through four or five octaves
in the Madhouse on Madison, Marvin Gaye toning it up

in the Forum) and rappers and crooners—but
nothing remotely like this one. And no one's

got clue number two how he does this.
"Hey, all I do is play it," he says

a week or so later on Dick Cavett.
"I'm American so I played it. They made me sing it

in school, so it's sort of a flashback."
Cavett, flashing us forward to his slick

Nineties self as a blandly narcissistic
middlebrow pitchman, waxes sarcastic:

"This man was in the 101st Airborne,
so when you write your nasty letters in—"

Hendrix, baffled, asks, "Nasty letters? How come?"
Cavett: "When you mention the national anthem

played in any unorthodox way, it never fails.
You get a guaranteed percentage of hate mail

from people who say 'How dare he?' " Hendrix
(still baffled): "Unorthodox? It wasn't unorthodox."

Cavett: "It wasn't unorthodox?" Hendrix: "No.
I thought it was beautiful, but there you go."

He shoots the camera a rightside up, then
upside down, not unbelligerent, peace sign. . . .

The upshot? Whenever we witness the national anthem
because a war is about to get started

fought by soldiers in camouflage or surrogate warriors
in eyecatching uniforms, we have to think of Jimi.

29

According to Professor Richard S. Wrong, "The United States
has clung to a naive belief in the unquestioned virtues
of a free world market way way too long after the loss
of its postwar economic dominance, and despite the manifest
        failure
of Japan and Europe to fucking practice laissez-faire, either
internationally or domestically." Professor Wrong further
        contends
that the combined effect of the "asshole" Japanese and European
revival in the 1960s, together with domestic American inflation
resulting from the war in Vietnam, so weakened the dollar
that its "old boy" position as an international unit of exchange
forced Sir Richard M. Nixon to abandon the Bretton Woods
exchange-rates agreements in 1970; the dollar henceforward

would float. Concerning the still pending case of Irmen
v. Wrzesinski, Wrong could not be reached for comment.

30

I was hustling north on Michigan Avenue
headed for Tale of the Whale, where DB
had scheduled the shoot and our interview.
With the windchill it must've been 20

or 25 below out, but the sidewalks were crowded
with bundled-up lunch-hour shoppers. At the corner
of Superior the signal turned red and I stopped.
A skinny young black kid, maybe thirteen or

fourteen, kept walking. He was wearing the new
black Air Pippens and a red vinyl windbreaker.
He was trying to make it across Superior
ahead of the traffic, but he still didn't seem

to be in all that much of a hurry. Not him.
As he reached the middle of the street
his left foot shot over his head like
he was following through on a punt. Both arms

went sideways, and his other foot slid out
from under him. He flailed in midair for a couple
three seconds, frantically grabbing for help,
balance—something. No dice. He came down real hard

on his butt, actually bounced a few inches,
then sat on the asphalt. By this point the cars
in both westbound lanes were almost on top of him
and a woman next to me on the curb started screaming.

The drivers, however, had managed to stop
without hitting him. The kid had his back to me
now, so I couldn't see the look on his face.
What I could see was the three-foot strip

of slick, icy snow that had got him. He was practically
sitting on top of it. Aside from this one single patch,
the asphalt was dry as a bone.
                              The kid slowly picked himself up.
He grinned at the two lines of cars that had formed

then threw back his shoulders and puffed out his chest.
It was strange. Right arm in front of his waist, left arm
behind him, he bowed deeply to the traffic, his weird,
asymmetrical haircut just about brushing
against one of the bumpers. Horns started blaring.
One of the drivers swerved past, shouting obscenities
at the kid and flipping him off through the windshield.
The kid just ignored this. He turned to the people
on the opposite sidewalk and bowed for a second time.
Two more cars rocketed past him, blasting their horns
and angling deliberately close. Still taking his time,
the kid spun around on his heel, faced my side of Superior,
and bowed once again. People shivering there with me

stared back at him, or glanced at each other,
but there was nothing we could think of to say.
Dodging a Honda, the kid finally sprinted off
in the same direction he'd been headed in the first place,
disappearing up ahead into the crowd of pedestrians.
The light turned green for the rest of us at exactly this moment.

31

Crosscountry skiers were cruising the beach as I jogged
along Sheridan Road, stutterstepping my way
past bundled-up couples just walking,

getting passed by the people on mountain bikes, all of us
getting these stiff little whiffs of diesel
and premium as we gaped at the black-

and-white landscape. That morning, in the bright dead
center of January, it had snowed for six hours;
there'd been almost no wind. Now snow

was everywhere, heaped grain by flake seven, eight
inches high along gutters and branches,
phone lines and bumpers. Even twigs

balanced miniature drifts steep in precarious cross-
section, crooked, impossibly vertical . . .
Rounding the bend where the white

granite juice-squeezer dome of the Baha'i Temple
rises up over Peter Jans Community Golf Course,
the fourth and fifth fairways bunkered

by drifts three feet deep tracked by skis, kids in boots,
I remembered again: we were going to war.
I ran home and turned on the news.